Back to Babylon

Palewell Press

Back to Babylon

Agnes Meadows

Back to Babylon

First edition 2019 from Palewell Press, www.palewellpress.co.uk

Printed and bound in the UK

ISBN 978-1-911587-20-0

A CIP catalogue record for this title is available from the British Library.

Acknowledgements

I would particularly like to acknowledge the extraordinary Dr Ali Al-Shalah, who set up the Babylon International Poetry & Arts Festival in 2012, and who invited me to attend that first Festival, plus the subsequent Festivals in 2014 and 2016. The Festival is still going strong, and showcases the work of poets, writers and artists from all over the world, thanks to Dr Ali's incredible energy and foresight in ensuring that poetry and art flourish despite Iraq's troubled past. I would also thank international oud player Ahmed Mukhtar, also an Iraqi, who first introduced me to Dr Ali and the Festival, and who has been a source of tremendous inspiration as a human being and an exceptional musician. Finally, thank you to Camilla Reeve who runs Palewell Press, for wanting to publish the poetry I wrote about my visits to Iraq, and the things I saw there.

Dedication

I dedicate this collection of work based on the three Arts &
Literature Festivals that I attended in Babylon to all the men,
women and children in the Babylon region who died as a result
of invasion, despotism and warfare in that troubled region. May
their souls rest peacefully, and may that tired and broken country
rise from the ashes to know the peace and growth it merits.

Contents

2012

Young Dancers in Babylon

In a night turbulent with expectation and flying things,
On stage five young girls in terrible frilly frocks dance
To the backdrop of oud under a watchful sky, a full moon sitting
Fat and silent as a reluctant bride. They dance, this pre-pubescent
Stripling quintet, untidy and joyous, their tiger's eye glances bright,
Knowing they are on the brink of wonder, of remarkable journeys,
Laughter curling their mouths like rosebuds waking, a condition
Of being that has been forgotten too long in the aftermath of conflict.

They dance, arms akimbo, dip and whirl, harvesting the
Applause of date-eyed boys, of mothers who spent half
A lifetime gestating patience and forgiveness, of old men
Who witnessed an excess of woe yet could still be moved by
Innocence and poetry. On the crenellated walls of this new
Amphitheatre, soldiers watch and listen, their Kalashnikovs slung
Forgotten across their shoulders, clapping to the rhythm of
Words and music, breathing in a new vocabulary of freedom.

Aftershock

This is no ordinary silence you are hearing. This is the silence
Of aftershock, when continents in collision, complete their slow
Rumble of destruction, and only the smell of corruption remains.

This is the silence of tyranny, of domination without mercy, of cruelty
That swears vengeance. It is that state of being between states of
Being, invisible to the naked eye, though not to the naked heart.

In that hypnogogic moment, whole universes
Collapse, white stars implode, the history of millennia
Erased from one breath to the next.

Inhale	civilizations flourish,
Exhale	a million mothers give birth.

Inhale	civilisations grow greedy,
	become fat and overburdened with bile.
	Secrets submerge in the eyes of prisoners
	who have personified the unimaginable.
	The camera bears witness to unseen torment.

Exhale	a million mothers watch their offspring
	stumble blindly in a sunless desert.
	Nobody hears their whispered despair.
	Their hearts no longer function.
	They are the living dead.

And in between
A thread of sound is born
Connecting silence to silence.

This is the eye of the storm.

Between one breath and the next

How would you feel, English, if you sent your son to
Buy bread and he didn't come back? How would you feel if,
After hours had passed, you walked the streets calling his name
In case he was laying somewhere, misplaced, waiting for rescue,

For retrieval like a shoe that had fallen from the wearer's foot
Unheeded, lost now in the mire at the roadside, scarred by
Wind and weather. And at midnight, when he had still not
Returned, and the dreadful knocking of tears that threatened to

Scythe you open, remained trapped behind the locked door of
Your eyes, a tsunami of stone and boulder, and you did not
Know where else he might be sought, how would you feel?

How would you feel, if you saw blood on the ground,
Each droplet no longer brilliant, as if the sun had already set
In each corpuscle, and you followed the train of crimson beads
Serrating the pavements, your heart a helicopter beat in your breast,

Your eyes handcuffed to the ground, imprisoned by your own
Fear and anger, the clamor of gunfire in the distance marking
Midnight's invasion, shrouding your tears, the palms of your hands
Wet with desperation, the ache in your breast an echo of birth-pangs.

And you had stopped calling his name into the unraveling darkness,
For you had run out of breath, your throat raw, your mouth filled
With the ashes of hope. My boy, my beautiful boy, the clamor of
Devotion still in his eyes… my son.

How would you feel, English,
If all of this was known to you
Between one breath and the next?

Lion

In this country of ruins and ruination,
In the shadow of the dead dictator's palace,
Babil's stone lion crouches, toothless and alone,
Features worn smooth by the touch of
Millennia and civilisation's careless hands,
The relentless sun stronger than lies.
And from among the ancient dun-coloured bricks
And unhappy palms, the call to prayer
Sifts in shifting sibilance, its edges sharp
As breaking glass, a subtle reminder
That this time of tragedy will also pass.

Misunderstanding

We smile in tentative greeting. They do not smile back,
These old crow women, fully hijabbed and shapeless,
Scandalized by our white arms, our shameless faces,
Our heathen hair, every inch of us open to the sky,
Uncovered and blatant.

There is suspicion in their eyes, telling us
They will guard their sons, and daughters too;
They will guard their monuments, their dusty history;
They will guard their tongues, will not speak, stay mute
And untouched by the conspiracy of lies that have

Consumed their heritage and homeland with greedy mouths,
The ruination that we, unwitting, represent. There are unasked
Questions trapped within each down-turned mouth,
Our motivation suspect, our presence an affront.
They wait for us to remove the mask of sisterhood,

To steal what is not ours, like every other of our kind,
Leaving only poverty and decay, a black hole of despair
That will never be filled, not while they live, nor their sons,
Nor their grandsons. And we know that our poetry,
Though it is redolent with compassion, will never compensate,

That nothing we write or say will ever be sorry,
Not one word will ever be sorry enough.

Marigolds

There is dust covering the moon, and the stars
Have fled to safety. On the bank of the Euphrates,
Old Mother River, grown grey and sluggish with indifference,
There are marigolds for sale, thousands cascading along
The cracked paving stones and gutters, their gilded faces
Gleaming in the soft-pleated dusk, a vibrant living coinage
Echoing an ancient gardener's lasting dream of beauty
Sustained in the face of so much death.

Small Poem

Under a silent moon the poets cry in words
Of storm and thunder. Under a spare tree in the dark,
Dr Ali's son grasps his bottle in fierce fat little fingers,
Sucks avidly, onyx bright eyes agleam with
Satisfaction, the bud of his mouth furled in
Silent contentment. A small poem written with love.

At Nemrut's Tower of God

Soldiers stand in clusters at Nemrut's Tower of God,
Festooned with the machinery of conflict. Though they
Have been trained to blank emotion, they have a way of
Standing that arias machismo, their bodies upright and
Muscular, the dignity of the flame burning fiercely within them.

Our presence ignites their curiosity, as if we have been
Conjured by *djin,* an unexpected mirage, a pod of poets alien
As dolphins in this oasis of faith. The hours of grey, smothering
Boredom blow away from them, back into the desert,
Settling finally among the rip-tide of palm-trees
That ocean the horizon all the way to Babylon.

These boy-men guard this place of pilgrimage against looters or
Fanatics, the holy man's blue tiled tomb frilled with the grubby lace
Of contemporary detritus, with rusted Coke tins, plastic bags,
And sweet-wrappers winking and fidgeting under midday's abrasive
Scouring sun, one man's folly manifest in brick and stone,
God's words carved invisibly in dust and stillness.

They watch us in ill-concealed amusement; follow us as we
Stumble towards ruins that finger a bleached and blistered sky,
Help me across the steep sand-blasted paths, past archaic doorways,
Breached remnants of hearth or kitchen, hold my hand with masculine
Firmness, photograph us all with adolescent zeal, declining to return
The favor with a reluctant wagging finger. "It is forbidden," they say,
Smiles remaining dormant in their oil-dark eyes.

And over the brown earth, the broken walls, the split open homes
In which voices have long been silent; over the dead gardens,
Smoke rising from oil fires in the distance, the litter-collaged stalls
Selling water and cheap snacks; over the desiccation of old women
Sitting bird-quick in the relentless sunlight, scratching their hearts
To see if the blood still flows in limbs made powerless by lost dreams
And mutated hopes; over the compassionless land that has nothing

Left to give, where even the trees are tired as they huddle round
Scum-filled pools like rusted tanks; over the raven-winged specter
Of the dead saint picking at the bones of the living, removing the final
Trivial fragments of adoration still threading devotion's ruptured
                                        sinews;
Over all these things, the voice of the muezzin surges,
Rippling the tide of air on air in unhurried swell.

On a morning in May at Al-Mawahil, near the City of Al-Hillah

Al-Mawahil is a mass grave of 13,000 disappeared Iraqis, including women and children, missing since 1991, butchered by Saddam Hussein. It is near Babylon, Iraq.

No gravestones embossed with the names of
Loved ones, nor photographs grown pale with
Seasonal passage, nor flowers, nor any sense of peace
Or rest, just numbered wooden markers, row upon
Row as far as the eye could see, corn rows of death
By the roadside at Al-Mawahil, near the City of the Hill,
Not far from Babylon, with the traffic muttering in an
Angry sub-text, and ten thousand un-named spirits
Howling underground, a banshee wail reflecting the cry
Of mothers rendered unreasonable by grief's weight.

Have you ever seen a woman so torn apart by woe
That her mouth has become a gaping wound, her lips
Drawn thin over her teeth in a parody of laughter,
Her eyes blinded now with anguish? And the noise
Escaping from the prison of her broken features is no longer
Human, her head thrown back as she becomes breathless
And gasping, the animal shriek of agony going on and on,
On and on, on and on and on, replicating endlessly until

It takes the skin off your heart in compassion, and every part
Of you vibrates with the harshness of it, a raw relentless
Kind of pain. And you're praying that it will stop, like she
Is praying that it will stop, for the comfort of lies, for the
Yesterday when this kind of grief was not a word in her
Dictionary of loss, when her child, her brother, father, sister,
Mother, husband, neighbor, friend, was not reduced to an
Occasional limb, unidentifiable, dismembered, disappeared, but
At her side, warm and vibrant in the moon-smile of evening.

If you have never seen that woman in her mantle of despair,
Then you will not know what I saw on that morning in May
At Al-Mawahil, near the city of Al-Hillah, not far from Babylon,
Nor will you understand why I stood still and cried.

2014

Riverbank

An early evening sun gilds the unwrinkled jade water
Of Babil's river as it slides by in silk smooth silence,
Its banks adorned with a kaleidoscopic frieze of
Marigolds and Jasmine flower. Close by, poets necklace
Words of fire and blood in scarlet threads, competing
With the voice of the muezzin as he fingers heaven.
Both speak of a God hidden beneath layers of sand
And avarice, while swallows swoop and plummet,
Snatching sequins of emerald water by the beak-full,
Before flickering, bat-like, away into the lowering dusk.

Summer Palace in Babil

Red azaleas cascade down the hill
From the garden of the despot's summer palace,
Each glowing scarlet petal a drop of blood
Drawn from the hearts of a thousand thousand
Children, and their mothers, and their fathers,
A waterfall of bright, living gore spilled onto
Babil's dumb, indifferent ground.

Inside the deserted mansion, time worn now and
Crumbling, its walls graffitied with the names of lovers
So young they had never known heart-break, there, even
At noon, with the sun shining in unrelenting power, shadows
Still congregate in restless clusters, fearful and whispering,
Like anxious leaves caught in a burgeoning tempest.

And if you listen carefully, eyes closed, breath held fast,
You can still hear the great leader's pitiless laughter
Threading through the darkness, all that remains of his cruel
Control, concealing the anguished cries of a nation in hell,
Mourning its lost youth, its lost past, its yesterdays of sorrow.

Under the Lotus Tree

Each day for decades, the woman sat beneath the
Lotus tree, silent in the dust and debris, her head
Bowed, eyes closed, her skin grey as old candle-wax,
Hands flaccid in her lap as if they had forgotten
How to hold or touch, for she had been forbidden
To speak, to question or refuse, forbidden even
To feel in the war-zone of her days, bound by the gag
Of custom, dogma, and of ignorance, the effects of
Conflict, layer upon layer of unacknowledged loss
And sadness, a desperation of fear stitching her
Soul with dark threads, sewing her lips tight shut.

In her world, everyone had had a gun, and everyone
Had used it; everyone hunted and was hunted,
Everyone pretended nothing was wrong. This was
How it had always been, would always be, without
Respite. It was a heavy load she carried unprotesting,
As if its weight was of no consequence, as if it would
Make no difference, as if her back would not be broken,
Her heart would not be shattered, a pane of glass
Splintering in the sonic boom of unyielding tyranny.

And then one morning, quite suddenly in the hour before
Daybreak, when sunlight glowed blood-red on the rim of
The world, her eyes opened into the dawn of realisation,
Her fists clenched in her lap remembering their function at last,
And, head raised high in rediscovered pride, she opened
Her mouth, and such a shriek of anger, frustration and despair
Burst from her lips, whole cities trembled, mountains cracked
Wide open, turned to dust and rubble, rivers changed their
Course, and even the air grew black with bile.

"Enough," she shrieked. "Enough!"

The lotus tree commemorates the lost.

Light Within Light

Each day, when we find him, the old man has dirt in his mouth,
Oil black and gritty, as if he has been speaking directly into
The ground, communicating with the roots of trees, with earthworms,
Centipedes, or the bones of broken things. His words are disfigured
By grime and gravel, each one turned to mud in the oasis of his lips,
Names repeated again and again, every syllable snagged by
Silent weeping, a mute caravanserai of tears watering his cheeks,
Of tears watering his cheeks, a mantra of despair we cannot fathom.

They told me he had been a gardener in the old days
Before the madness started; that he was accustomed
To the feel of the living earth under his fingers; that he
Spoke to each shoot and leaf as if it was a child, nurturing
Them as they grew, quick with pride, a job well done.

They told me he had fathered a daughter, one priceless child,
More dear to him than sunrise, cherished her like a tree, his own
Orchard of hope; that whenever he said her name, it was as if
The Grace of God had blessed his lips, his precious flower,
His Yasmina, light within light, the very fruit of love.

They told me when she disappeared, taken by the despot's henchmen,
He became mad with grief, left his home, his wife, his gardens,
Walked shoeless from town to town, face etched deep with
Anguish and confusion, stopped every night to ask each passing
Stranger if they had seen a child, a lost child, not yet ten, with eyes
The colour of amber lit from behind by sunlight, growing slowly into
Girlhood, tall and slender as a sapling.

And the days passed, and the weeks turned to years, and his
Barefoot walk continued, town after town, his questioning never
Changing nor ceasing: "Have you seen a child, not yet ten?
"My Yasmina, my precious flower, growing slowly into womanhood,
"Straighter than a lotus tree."

But no-one answered him, not once in all the years of his wandering,
Until at last the old man spoke directly into the earth itself,
His fractured voice murmuring over the bones of broken things,

Past the nameless, faceless thousands who had been buried
In secret haste, ten deep by the roadside, during the long years
Of war and tyranny, their limbs torn and tangled in the untidy
Asymmetry of death. Each night his lips still murmur words of love
To his lost child, his Yasmina, precious flower of his heart,
Light within light. And every day when we find him, his mouth is
Filled with dirt, oil black and gritty, a kiss on the face of torment.

What Came First

After the terrorist attacks in various parts of Europe

First there was the taste of fear,
Neither sweet nor sour,
But ash-acrid, a deep-throated bitterness
Burning and heavy, covering everything.

Even before the sound of gunfire had
Embroidered an evening where only
Autumn leaves had helter-skeltered,
Dream-driven and vulnerable, rain
Scratching windowpanes and passing cars
With November's spiteful fingernails;

Even before the angry rip of winnowing bullets,
The overwhelming wrench of grenade bellow,
Or soul's implosion sifting through the brain's
Synaptic passageways, a million particles of despair,
Futile and inelegant, slicing away all thoughts of
Graceful tomorrows, effortlessly cutting to the bone;

Even before the heightened crimson wetness
Of blood, a red kite dancing in the hurricane
Of night-time terror, flowering bench and table,
Spraying limbs that lay like broken skittles now
Scattered and defunct, no longer functional,
No longer attached, the music of the day submerged

Beneath hatred's shouted rhetoric,
Impaling tongues and hearts,
Making a lie of faith. Before
All these things, there was
Fear.

2016

Lingua Franca in Babylon

In the lavish hotel built by Saddam on Babil's ruined outskirts,
In the shadow-bruised rooms now used for wedding celebrations,
We gather under a chandelier the size of Paris.

A brutal collection of gilded guns in golden frames decorates
Its walls, the extravagantly carved chairs we sit upon, thrones
Carved to flatter the long-dead tyrant's monumental ego.

We are the added condiment in this rich broth of Festival words,
A Turk, a German, two Argentinians, and me, a Londoner,
The palest of this quintet of poets, Spanish our *lingua franca*.

Smiling, I acknowledged the irony of it, for, far distant
From the relentless messages of guns and grief, woe and warfare,
Broadcast daily from this ancient land to a war-hungry world,

We communicate in the language of humanity, the plangent poetry
Of brotherhood, ours an unvoiced commitment to truth and beauty.
And if there are any differences between us, it is because, after all,

We are only human.

Habibi

Thoughts of an ordinary Babylonian husband.

Rest your hands upon my face, habibi, for just a moment longer.
There is so little time to wonder if our sons or our daughters
Will make us proud. Instead, take this moment as a gift.
Come lay beside me now beneath the bullet-pocked window
Of our home. Breathe in the quietness of stars. Let my love
And the moon's pallid face, do battle with your fear.

I will remove the smell of fire from your skin,
Transform it to sweet burning, to frankincense, to freedom.
Disregard what comes stealing through these crumbling walls,
For it is not gunfire you hear, nor the whirr of helicopter blades;
It is the sound of my heartbeat, the echoes of gladness as I bid you
Welcome, for I am a house without locks, open only to you.

Use your love as a map-maker charting the geography
Of consummation, inking new territories of joy onto
The blank parchment of my heart. And when it becomes too hard
To recall the contentment of our life together, let me wipe away
The cobwebs of suffering that entangle us both, so that you may
Sleep unchallenged, and your face can reclaim its treasury of hope.

The Request

*An injured Iraqi soldier's request while at supper at the Babylon
International Arts & Cultural Festival*

He approached us with diffidence, a young Iraqi soldier, his right arm
Scaffolded with steel rods and ugly metal screws holding flesh
And bone together, his fingers swollen and useless in a cradle
Of bandages stained with old blood, his skin patterned purple and
Brown with the sickle marks of death avoided by a hair's breadth.

He was barely an adult, 20 maybe, or 21, his military hair-cut
Grown ragged now, less formal. Yet already he had seen a
Lifetime's death and destruction, the memory of horror barely
Submerged on his unremarkable face, subcutaneous recollections
Of fallen comrades scarring his soul, the echoes of bomb-blast
And gun-fire an internal nightmare reverberating endlessly in
A silent, tortured white noise of the heart.

But that night, coming to our supper table, a starling flock
Of foreign poets and performers brought to Babylon for art's sake,
There was fear in his eyes, genuine and undiluted. It stopped us
In our tracks, halting our conversation, making us question what
He feared, for we were little more than an ostentation of creative
Peacocks for whom war was just a newspaper headline,
Not a personal wolf-howl reality, and only our words were explosive.

His reality was different, his arm fragmented by a roadside bomb,
The razor blade of death shaving him so close, he was the only
Survivor of an attack too commonplace to make the evening news.
They'd pieced him together like a second-rate jigsaw missing
Crucial parts before the picture could be whole again. Now, weeks
Later, he stood before us, dredging up shrunken reserves of courage,
panic bleaching his eyes, while we wondered what he wanted.

Breaking into our puzzled silence at last, he cleared his throat
And asked, in a voice barely audible above the restaurant chatter,
If he could be photographed with us, if we wouldn't mind, if it wasn't
Disturbing us. It would be a source of pride, he said, if he could
Stand in our midst, show his Mother a picture of him surrounded by
Poets instead of one where he was weighed down with the grim
Paraphernalia of conflict, beside the rubble of combat-crushed
Homes and carnage-stained alleyways.

His humility shamed us all, for we had only ever known comfort,
Without a single day of battle-brought loss or lack, so that, as one,
We reached out to him in welcome, this modest young man,
With his unremarkable face and ragged hair, telling him we'd be
Proud to be photographed standing at his side. And when he saw us
Again two nights later at the well-thumbed down-town
Hospitality Palace restaurant, he approached us as friends,
Without fear, with only smiles and awkward handshakes.

There are many things about life in that ancient city
That have made me cry. The memory of that young soldier's
Fear and friendship is just one of them.

Baghdad Blog

A diary of my time in Iraq as a guest and participant at the first Babylon International Festival of Arts & Cultures – 04-11 May 2012

DAY ONE – Morning, 4th May – On the Way to Babylon

We circle Baghdad airport in the early morning, sky dull with the beginnings of a sandstorm. It is impossible to see more than a few yards ahead with any clarity, buildings, trees, and people all blurred with a blanket of dust blown in from the desert that comprises most of this country. As soon as I step off the 'plane my eyes and nose start to itch, and before long I am sneezing.

No hassle getting into Iraq; I hope getting out will be equally unproblematic. I'm met by the Festival driver (who speaks no English), and we drive through the outskirts of Baghdad as a tired sun trudges wearily higher in the grit-filled sky. There is a heavy military presence – not just soldiers with machine guns, but armored cars with all the paraphernalia of 'protection', tanks, and barbed-wire topped concrete walls with gun turrets every few hundred yards. I try not to feel nervous, but looking at the ruins of a city that has been completely flattened by decades of war, it's easy for my already over-active imagination to run away with me.

The driver weaves slowly through the rubble-strewn streets. He is silent, and I am both too tired and too shaken to speak. He takes me to his house, a low-roofed gated building that has seen better days. Inside there is a flat-screen tv, a computer, heavy blood-colored furniture, and photographs of solemn-eyed people I will never meet decorating the walls. I am invited to sit, given water to drink.

After what seems like an eternity I am joined by other participants in the Festival, Fatma Naoot, a young Egyptian journalist and writer from Cairo, and Moammal Ekrema, a Syrian calligrapher from Damascus. A lavish breakfast of pitta, humus, eggs, cheese, and carrot jam is spread before us, but I'm too tired to eat, aware that my refusal of hospitality is considered discourteous. It's good to meet Moammal and Fatma, whose

English is excellent, and once again I'm ashamed I can barely say hello and thank you in Arabic. For a while we talk Egyptian politics, and then at 11.00 a.m. we set off at last – I've been up for 27 hours and my brain hurts.

I try not to be overwhelmed by the immensity of what I'm seeing. This town is a broken ruin, more broken than you could possibly imagine, every single building wrecked, streets piled high with the rubble of endless conflict, and heaps of rubbish everywhere. This is a city that has had its heart ripped out and the fragments scattered, so that streets, neighborhoods - all the normal signs of life that I'm used to seeing as the sun stretches into another day - are barely recognizable here. But there are people here, human beings trying their hardest to have a life, and that's what I've come to see.

On the 'plane there were men and women with their young children, returning home. I felt reassured if children are being brought back, I think. Despite the destruction, despair, the wreckage and the fear and pain written on the faces of everyone, there must be the tiniest shoot of hope that things might actually get better eventually. Perhaps the Festival is part of that slow, incredible revival. I hold onto that fragile hope as we continue the 80-kilometer drive through the sand-blasted landscape all the way to Babylon.

DAY ONE – Evening, 4th May – Arriving in Babylon

Finally arrive in Babylon around noon, the aftermath of the sandstorm still evident in the orange colored sky and layer of fine dust covering everything. The hotel complex I am to call home for the next few days has definitely seen better days, with bungalow-style blocks of rooms set amongst threadbare gardens where roses struggle to lift their sorry heads.

There doesn't seem to be a plan or programme, but at this stage I'm too tired to worry about it, convinced that someone will tell me what's happening and introduce me to everyone else later. Besides, from other visits to the Middle East and Asia, I've learned to go with the flow and take casual management in my stride. All will be revealed – eventually.

My room is enormous, filled with a suite of extraordinary bedroom furniture. The bed itself is about the size of the average Parisian 'bijou' apartment, and could easily sleep four people, six if they were thin! Bed, wardrobe, and chest of drawers are all in elaborately carved dark wood, heavily decorated with white metal, so bizarre I have to take photos. The room has everything it should have – fridge, phone, wall clock, tv, aircon/fan. Unfortunately, only the tv is working, stuck on National Geographic without sound, plus the lugubrious fan (a blessing as it's 40 degrees outside).

It is also unquestionably the filthiest room I've ever stayed in, a layer of grit covering the grimy carpet, making walking barefoot hazardous. The bed linen on the gigantic bed is torn and stained – I don't want to think about what with – and the bathroom is a cavernous, mucky room covered in cracked medicinal pink tiles. The toilet doesn't flush, a squadron of fierce mosquitoes hovering around me as I take a shower in the sunken pit that doubles as a shower cubicle. But the water is hot and plentiful, which is all I need right now. A hot shower and then sleep for a few hours lying on top of the bed, covering myself with one of my shawls so the mossies don't eat my feet.

I wake at 5.00 p.m. The sun is still high in the sandy sky, and I'm beginning to think food might be nice. I eat the nuts I saved from the 'plane, have another shower then leave my room to find where everyone else is. Not a soul in sight, just a few surly gardeners watering the rose-beds, their eyes busy with curiosity and unasked questions. I say hello. They ignore me. I walk around for 15 minutes, see no-one. The 'office' is closed. Still no indication of a programme. So I go back to my room, watch more mute National Geographic, doze until 8.00 p.m. then try again, wondering if the Festival organisers have forgotten I'm here. The sun has set, the night is turbulent with flying things and there is the heady smell of jasmine in the air.

Determined to find someone who can tell me what's going on, I head back to the 'office' where a cluster of middle-aged mono-eyebrowed men in grey suits sit watching tv and smoking cigarettes. They greet me effusively, usher me in, offer me cold drinks, insist on taking 'photos on their mobiles of us together. On the coffee table in front of them is a pistol, and I know each of them carries his own weapon under his jacket. I make a feeble joke about guns. Nobody laughs; for them, carrying a gun is normal, even at a poetry/arts festival. I couldn't be further away from the Poetry Café if I tried!

Half an hour passes, still nothing happens, and I begin to get impatient. I ask again where everyone is and what's programmed for tonight. At last someone calls Dr Ali Al-Shalah, the Festival's hard-working Director, who invited me to attend after we'd met at a poetry festival in Zurich. Much rapid-fire conversation ensues and within minutes I'm dispatched into the night in a cab.

By the time I arrive at the Festival's launch event in an open air amphitheatre, the programme is almost over. At the door I see Dr Ali and he greets me effusively, as happy to see me as I am to be seen. I'm led to my seat where several of the other foreign writers are sitting – Lasse Soderberg and Angela Garcia from Sweden, Jona and Tobias Burghardt from Germany, Lisa Mayer from Austria and Aminur Rahman from Bangladesh. They smile and shout their hello's cheerfully; I've rarely been greeted with such warmth by complete strangers, and I start relaxing in the enthusiasm of their reception.

On stage a troupe of pretty primary-school age girls in frilly frocks with matching hats are performing a simple but lively dance. When they finish, the applause is thunderous, and they giggle and kiss their hands at the audience like seasoned troupers. On the crenellated walls of this new amphitheatre, a bevy of soldiers listen to oud and poetry, clapping to the rhythm of the words, the AK47's that are slung casually over their shoulders forgotten for now. Before I came here someone said to me that poetry didn't seem appropriate in a war zone. I had replied that surely that's when poetry is needed most. What I'm witnessing now, under a watchful moon, surely proves my point.

Another few moments and the performances are over, and all the guest writers are shepherded onto a bus to take us back to the hotel complex where dinner awaits us. We dine al fresco, talk and laugh, poets and writers from so many places drawn together by our common love of words and the conviction that war and occupation are never the solution to anything. I'm glad I'm here, glad to be part of this Festival and all that it represents. Later, I fall asleep to the mute flicker of more National Geographic on the tv, the insistent whine of murderous mosquitoes.

DAY TWO – Saturday, 5th May – Morning - An Ancient City in a Despot's Shadow

During the night I am sure I must have lost at least an armful of blood, the mosquitoes were so prolific, so relentless and so hungry. Sleep was spasmodic and restless, partly because my imagination was on overdrive and I kept dreaming there were dreadful faceless things prowling around in the shrubbery outside our rooms. In the light of day and over breakfast I learn that this isn't too far from the truth, as Saddam Hussein had ordered the construction of this hotel complex and the gardens it stood in. When he was ousted, the place closed down and had only recently re-opened – no wonder it is looking so shabby!

Not only that, the dictator's summer palace is perched on a hill overlooking the hotel, literally a stone's throw away…a chilling thought that we were sleeping in the shadow of a despot's palace even though it is boarded up and no visitors are allowed in. Lisa, the Austrian writer, confessed that she got up very early and walked up the hill to take a closer look, but only got as far as the outside of the palace walls before being stopped by armed police and soldiers. She said the atmosphere up there was eerie and unpleasant, like a stone on the heart.

After breakfast, and still with absolutely no idea what the day's programme had in store for us, we compare notes on impressions so far. All of us agree that Dr Ali has done/is doing an amazing job and that this Festival is a really important landmark for Iraq and its strife-torn people. That we are here at all is a tribute to him and the people he is working with. The first few days will be devoted to literature, with readings by the European/International poets and writers, as well as the Arab poets drawn from Egypt, Syria, Turkey and from all over Iraq.

There are also exhibitions of contemporary visual arts and calligraphy. Maami's work is exhibited and is incredibly beautiful…even though I don't truly appreciate the calligrapher's art, I can recognize high quality when I see it, and his work is extraordinary. Later on in the week there will be film screenings and theatre/dance productions and the Festival will culminate in a concert by the Baghdad Symphony Orchestra. I wish I could to stay for the whole week instead of just the first few days. I didn't even know Baghdad had a Symphony Orchestra. There's so much about this place we don't know, or have the wrong idea about.

Mid-morning, we are taken to the ancient city of Babylon, the ruins of which are on the other side of the hill Saddam Hussein's summer palace is perched on. It is only a five minute bus drive away, but nevertheless we are accompanied by armed guards and a bevy of what I later realize are plain clothes police – large unsmiling men in modern shiny suits and ties (always a bit of a give-away, especially at a poetry festival!). Dr Ali is making sure we aren't captured by the opposition political party to discredit what the current government is trying to achieve. Another comforting thought to keep me awake at night alongside the voracious mossies!

In the 6th Century BC Babylon was the greatest city in the then known world and the centre of culture, wealth and learning. Whether the Hanging Gardens were real or a myth, people from all over the ancient world were drawn to it for its architectural marvels and to worship at the feet of the stone lions of Babylon, symbols of supreme power and might. I am completely overawed that I am actually here.

Over 2,600 years ago the biblical King Nebuchadnezzar commissioned the construction of streets I am walking down now, had entered the magnificent (and magnificently restored) Ishtar Gate, one of the six gateways to the city, devoted to Ishtar, Goddess of love, war and fertility, as I am doing now. The gate is breathtaking, covered in luminous indigo tiles interspersed with images of hybrid animals, mixtures of birds, bulls, fish and fowl, and the ubiquitous lions, Ishtar's own symbol, all in brilliant yellow and white. Once inside there is a courtyard filled with stone benches, a cluster of palm trees, a mural of an ancient map of the world showing Babylon in the centre of things surrounded by ocean. An arrow points east to the Great Wall (of China), another saying it is 'six leagues in between where the sun is not seen."

It is easy to imagine the bustle and excitement of this city, this gateway in those far-away days when it really was the centre of the world and people flocked there to learn and to marvel. Now we are virtually the only visitors, certainly the only foreigners, apart from a thin sprinkling of Iraqi teenagers or families here to see the glories of their past. A few years ago there had been plans to restore the whole site and make it a major tourist attraction, but those plans have been shelved for some time now. In one corner of the courtyard is a dusty little shop with a sign saying 'Welcome – Souvenirs of Babylon' under which another sign says 'Closed.' To me it seems an incredibly poignant metaphor for the whole of Iraq. I came to Babylon and it was closed.

The temperature in the blistering sun is in the upper 40's, so hot it is an effort to breath. In the shade of the courtyard's palm trees an enterprising Iraqi has a stall selling cold drinks. We all look longingly at the box of ice-cold cola's and water, our tongues already glued to the roof of our mouths, but we can't buy anything not having any Iraqi currency. Once again, the kindness of local writers comes to our rescue, and we are all bought drinks, with much laughter and generosity of spirit, plus the eternal "where are you from?"

Walking through the sunbaked streets I am aware of the weight of millennia, each brick in those ancient walls a word in the book of silence. The city spreads out before us, an endless Escher landscape of dun-colored walls, broken doorways and roofless buildings that once must have been grand and beautiful.

When a wizened local elder points to the cuneiform inscriptions carved in some of the bricks, translating in a shy voice that these were made at the time of King Nebuchadnezzar, I get very excited. Well…I'm a history buff, so things this old and precious will always excite me. And this was the King Nebuchadnezzar, of biblical fame. How could that not be cool? It hurts my heart to think that all this history, the wealth of culture and beauty that is here, is largely hidden from us in the West. All we hear about is despotism, war, death and destruction, but this is only a part of what this country has to offer. How could we not be told about everything else? A rhetorical question, I know.

In one ruined courtyard we visit the Woman's Well, where your 'womanly sins' can be washed away. On the wall outside is a massive shadow clock pointing towards the dictator's palace with a lengthening dark finger. The stone lion sits alone amidst the ruins, its face worn by the hands of the careless, by rain and turmoil, now only a symbol of loss.

We are quiet when we get back on the bus to return to the hotel for lunch. History has a habit of silencing you, and we are all even more aware now of what there had once been and how much has been lost. My grubby room seems like a cool haven after the fierce heat and abrasive sunlight, and as I lay down for my post-lunch nap during the hottest part of the day, I wonder what other revelations this afternoon and evening's reading might bring. While I sleep, the mossies continue their relentless feasting.

DAY TWO – Saturday, 5th May – Afternoon – The Poetry of Loss

It's late afternoon when we get back on the bus to go to the first of the Festival's numerous readings, but it's still hotter than Hades. While we wait for latecomers, it gives us a chance to learn more about each other and to share our thoughts on poetry, books, travel and everything we've witnessed and are experiencing in this oven of a country. And I get the chance to practice my German with Lisa Mayer, and my much better Spanish with the lovely Colombian Angela Garcia (now living in Sweden with Lasse Soderberg, who has the driest sense of humor ever!), and the shining Jona Burghardt, originally from Argentina, now married to the ever-helpful German writer Tobias, from Stuttgart. We converse freely in a tangled mixture of English, German and Spanish, with a sprinkling of Arabic thrown in for added flavor. Every one of these people is a delight, and I keep reminding myself how lucky I am to be here with them.

At last we set off for our first event, a reading by some of the Iraqi and Arab writers attending the Festival. Following the bus is at least one fully armored vehicle complete with machine guns and significantly tooled up personnel. Our arrival at the open-air venue in the heart of the modern city of Babylon inspires a flurry of flak-jacketed soldiers and armed police to make sure we're well protected. Locals gawp as we get off the bus and walk into the compound on the banks of the River Euphrates. They're not used to seeing foreign civilians here, staring at us in blatant surprise. I've rarely felt so conspicuous or the object of such barefaced curiosity. But none of it's aggressive; they're just interested that foreigners want to come to their country for the pleasure of being there.

Entering the compound, a Book Fair that's also part of the Festival, is doing lively business. We are welcomed, given water, treated with respect, with endless requests for 'foto, foto.' Photos with children, proud parents, teenaged boys, young women, grandmothers in black headscarves and hijab, old men with the scars of loss engraved in their eyes, everyone wants to be photographed with us, and we all feel modestly proud - it would be easy to start believing your own publicity! But all these people are here for the love of the written and spoken word, and to share the memory of the outrage of grief and sorrow they have experienced.

One elderly woman reads from her manuscript, her voice wavering with emotion. There's something about her, her quiet dignity, the way she holds our attention with a soft voice. One of the Arab writers explains that she has written about her only son, who died on the last day of the war. How can she stand it, I think? How can she still greet us with a shy smile and a word of welcome? Lisa, Angela, Jona and I sought her out to thank her for her words, even though we hadn't understood them when she was reading. I wanted to hug her, but know this kind of physical contact is frowned upon, so I make do with a handshake, hoping that all the sympathy, compassion and sorrow at her loss will somehow travel through my fingertips into her hands and finally settle somewhere within her, that she will know that her grief has not gone unnoticed. It is a harsh moment.

The sun is beginning to set as we leave this first reading of the day. Dr Ali says we can go the next venue – an arts centre a couple of miles up the road - either on the bus or we can walk if we like. It isn't far, and the walk will take us through the Saturday market. A chance to walk through the market and see ordinary Iraqi's going about their business…no contest, we all agree!

So we set off along the crowded, car-filled streets of Babylon, with the moon rising and the plain clothes policemen following in our wake.

DAY TWO – Saturday, 5th May – Evening – Walking and Smiling in Babil

I'm pretty sure that when a lot of people think about the Middle East – if they think about it at all other than when the media reports conflict or despotism – they imagine the locals live in tents and get about on camels or donkeys. Or that they're a bunch of wild-eyed fanatics with tea towels on their heads and a Kalashnikov under each arm. Well, surprise, surprise – the truth is far, far away from this ignorant fantasy.

Babylon (Babil to the locals) is a modern city, albeit a battered and bruised one. It has traffic jams, cafes where men (and women) sit drinking coffee and eating cake, car show rooms with state of the art motors for those who can afford them, kiosks selling mobile 'phones and computer software, neon signs advertising banks and wedding dresses, and young people wearing blue jeans and trainers. And the people? Well, they're just trying to have a life, just like you and me, albeit after 40 years of despotism and war, so things are bound to be a little frayed around the edges.

Walking through the Saturday market is a real pleasure, and we all wish we could linger and look, talk to some of the people trying to make a living selling the thousand and one things you expect to find in a market. These are men and women with faces so sunburned they look as if they have been carved out of teak and then stained with coffee grounds, their hands gnarled as old tree roots, with decades of hard work and misfortune under their fingernails, scarring their cheeks. Yet seeing us among the luminous scarlet tomatoes and oranges the size of footballs (you won't get produce as fresh as that in your local Asda), they smile at our presence, the ever-present glimmer of curiosity in their eyes.

Lisa and I are both cross that we have no Iraqi currency to buy fruit or biscuits. There are these little bright green fruits that I think I recognize (called Erics) from my time in Turkey – unripe plums that are eaten with or without salt as an aid to digestion – that we are eager to taste. Dr Ali takes pity on us and treats us to a bagful. They are so sour they almost take the enamel off our teeth, and despite Dr Ali's generosity we both agree they are revolting.

The walk down that bustling street with the market stalls alive and busy is another high spot in a day of high spots. Again, the attention we are attracting just by virtue of our fair hair and skin, our foreign-ness, is extraordinary. Parents point us out to their staring children, and teenagers nudge each other in surprise and pleasure. Our faces begin to ache with the effort of smiling – after all we are cultural ambassadors of a sort. Sadly, some of the old women, dressed from head to foot in black with only hands and faces exposed, regard us with a greater degree of disapproval. They are not used to seeing bare-headed, bare-armed blondes who look them in the eye so boldly. All we can do is continue smiling. And anyway, I think I'm a bit long in the tooth to be considered a hussy!

The walk to the next event takes longer than expect, and by the time we get there I for one am purple with heat. Most of us Europeans are not going to be reading tonight, the majority of readers being the visiting Arab writers. Listening to the rise and fall of their voices, I reflect again what a beautiful language Arabic is, and how much poetry is respected and loved throughout the Arab world. This love isn't only for academics or intellectuals, but is evident at every level of Arab society. The audience includes many families with children who are actually paying attention, not fidgeting and yawning as they might do in the UK. Appreciation starts at an early age here, and poets are deemed special people – a nice change from being considered precious and irrelevant.

The moon is fat and full as we sit and listen to the poets speaking in voices of storm and thunder about things we will (hopefully) never know first-hand. Tomorrow it will be our turn to read. But for tonight all we have to do is listen and keep smiling under a waiting sky.

DAY THREE – Sunday, 6th May – Morning – At Nemrut's Tower, and the Graves of Al-Mawahil

By now all of us have given up on the idea there might be a written programme of events telling us what each day will hold. We've stopped fretting and are just going with the flow. This morning after breakfast we are taken to the tomb of a Muslim saint who built a tower so that he could speak more directly and easily to God. Nemrut's Tower of God is about an hour's drive away, giving us a chance to see more of the extraordinary countryside.

The landscape is a mosaic of dun-colored scrubland with ubiquitous palms standing like tired sentries, and an endless array of buildings split open by neglect or conflict, yet still with families living in them. Broken trees or fragments of rusted tanks lay scattered by the roadside. Occasionally there are the gated villas of the rich or powerful, as ostentatious and overblown as these types of dwellings usually are anywhere. What is self-evident, however, is that this is a weary land, one that has had the stuffing knocked out of it, a patchwork of decay and exhaustion filling me with sadness at the waste.

Arriving at the saint's tomb, we are quickly surrounded by a troupe of soldiers stationed there to keep away looters. In their dark blue uniforms, with hard muscular bodies and oil-dark eyes, they are a handsome bunch of boys, obviously delighted that the boredom of their days is to be alleviated for a little while by this posse of sightseeing poets who are tumbling from the bus like excited children. They all want to have their photos taken with us, but refuse to allow us to take photos of them, wagging their fingers and saying it is forbidden.

The tower stands a few hundred yards away up a steep hill that might once have had trees, but is now bare of all vegetation. Over centuries the village that had once thrived in the shadow of the saint's folly has fallen into ruin, now no more than a jumble of broken walls and doorways open to the cloudless sky. The earth is brown and stony, frilled with the detritus of 21st century living. A few tatty-looking stalls sell snacks and cold drinks, their ancient wizened owners eyeing us anxiously. People still live here although it is hard to imagine what kind of living they can scratch in such a remote and inhospitable place. In the distance an ocean of palm trees stretches in grey-green waves as far as the eye can see, smoke from distant fires pluming the horizon.

The others are much more determined to be tourists than me, with Lisa leaping up the steep slope to the crumbling tower that fingers the sky. I am happy to just stand and look at the eternity of trees spreading out before me, enjoying the chance to just <u>be</u> in this isolated spot. For a while there is only sunlight and silence, the hot air moving across the arid landscape as if God really is whispering in your ear. And then from the small blue-tiled mosque next to the saint's tomb, the muezzin calls the faithful to midday prayers. As ever I find it oddly moving and incredibly beautiful, his thin voice threading the emptiness to remind us of our impermanence. As we get back onto the bus, the onyx-eyed soldiers wave us goodbye, and the peace of the place travels with us for just a little while.

But Dr Ali has something in store for us that will erase all thoughts of peace and tranquility. He takes us to Al-Mawahil, the site of one of Saddam Hussein's most notorious mass-graves, where the remains of 13,000 men, women and children lay right next to a new housing estate. The newly built apartment blocks stand empty and waiting only yards away, with the steady thrum of motorway traffic connecting it to the graveyard. Corn-rows of unmarked graves stretch ahead, each one containing the partial remains of someone who had been butchered by Hussein for who knows what crime, real or imagined. These are the nameless 'disappeared', victims it has been impossible to identify as, often, only dismembered limbs remained.

On a billboard by the graveyard's entrance are pictures of women howling with grief, tearing at their hair and clothing in paroxysms of despair the depth of which I cannot even begin to imagine. Even my time in Gaza has not prepared me for this, and I am overwhelmed by a tsunami of sorrow for all those who were lost, and for those who have been left behind to mourn them. It is impossible for me not to cry, and we all stand in silence, joined by the anguish of the moment. Even now, writing about it weeks later, I can feel the ghost of the harsh emotion I felt seeing those graves, and the raw, savage grief that was being expressed by those weeping women. It was a cruel and shocking moment, but I'm glad I experienced it, for it was an unsubtle reminder how privileged our lives in the West really are.

We are all mute with distress as we return to Babylon, and lunch is a quiet affair, that silent shriek of woe still echoing somewhere in our heads.

DAY THREE – Sunday, 6th May – Afternoon/Evening – Poetry & Marigolds on the Euphrates

Our visit to Al-Mawahil has subdued us all, underlining our obligation as writers to report what we are witnessing in this broken country, and to write about our experiences. Otherwise what is the point of us coming? If we don't write about the Festival and what it represents, surely it will be just another literary ego trip, something unusual to add to our biographies? On the bus to the afternoon readings we can talk about little else, agreeing it has been a harsh and painful experience, yet an important one for us all to share. It helps to put Saddam Hussein's expulsion from power into perspective, whatever we feel or felt about the legitimacy of the war.

The Festival's Book Fair is still doing good business when we arrive there for the day's first readings later that afternoon. Each day we are given copies of the full-color newspaper supplements with photos of all of us sightseeing foreign writers, and translations in Arabic of the poems we submitted to the Festival. A young man takes a photograph of Jona, Alicia, Lisa and me smiling in front of a large Iraqi flag, which will appear in tomorrow's supplement. I meet the man who translated the two pieces I sent weeks ago, a delightful man called Hamid Al-

Shammari, who praises my work enthusiastically. He wants to put my poems on his website, together with photos of the two of us together… how can I refuse?

The afternoon erodes in a welter of heat and dust, the sun setting slowly in a flame-filled sky while more of the Arab writers read from their work. Even though most of us Europeans speak little or no Arabic, it is easy to understand the passion with which they read. Each has their own stories of brutality and bloodshed to tell, their writing providing a common platform of shared experience translates into the language of empathy. It is hard not to be moved by the emotion that is threaded through their words even if we cannot see the pictures they are creating.

As the moon rises sedately in an indigo sky, we transfer to the arts centre for the day's second readings, which will feature us Europeans (myself included). This time we travel by bus, and I for one am hugely grateful as the heat is still fierce enough to fry the top layer of skin clean off your body. The road from the Book Fare takes us along the banks of the Euphrates, one of the great rivers of the world, and I become quietly excited to be seeing it with my own eyes.

Enthusiasm aside, it saddens me this ancient river is so polluted, with rafts of rubbish floating near the riverbanks. All kinds of crap (literal as well as metaphorical) have welded into a messy carpet, a breeding ground for the voracious mosquitoes and evil-natured multi-legged bugs and beasties doubtless breeding there. I wonder why nobody cleans it up. There are piles of garbage accumulated everywhere – surely it would be more pleasant to live in a cleaner environment, and it wouldn't take much effort to clean it up?

But I recently learned that anyone trying to improve the look of where they lived would automatically be accused of getting above themselves, and be 'disposed' of, not exactly an incentive to develop an environmental conscience. Yet the spirit of those who created the legendary Hanging Gardens in ancient Babylon still lives in the modern city. Only inches away from the streams of evening traffic the riverbanks are transformed into one long garden centre with thousands of palms and marigolds for sale, a solid ribbon of green and gold foliage. It is strangely comforting to see the need to create beauty despite being in the midst of so much destruction.

Before the evening's readings we have a chance to look at some of the visual arts display and catch the exhibition of Moammal Ekrema's calligraphy. Each piece is a fluid and evocative masterpiece, a clear demonstration that Moammal is at the top of his game, a different kind of poetry. And then we begin to read our work – I am surprisingly nervous as I read my two poems. More photos ensue, more hand-shakes, more enthusiastic young people surrounding me for a group picture. You could get used to this, I think.

And then Dr Ali gets up on stage and in front of the entire audience describes how emotional I became when we'd visited Al-Mawahil that afternoon, and thanks me for crying. He actually <u>thanks me for crying</u>, for showing human compassion at a site of such monstrous inhumanity. Of course, that sets me off again, and soon I am surrounded by people taking pictures of me crying (not my best look!), which gets an even bigger round of applause. It's all a bit over-whelming. Fortunately, Jona, Lisa and Angela are at hand to cheer me up with their easy, undemanding friendship.

On the way back from the readings we stop for coffee at a roadside coffee shop in the heart of town. It's wonderful to sit in the open air watching young Babylonians relaxing and enjoying the pleasure of the moment. The coffee is sweet and strong enough to stop conversation, the night benign, and for that one moment conflict and death seems very far away.

DAY FOUR – Monday, 7th May – Morning - Interviews, Interviews, Interviews

Lisa left early this morning to return to her native Austria, but before she left she gave me the remainder of her mosquito spray. It has helped a little and I curse myself for not bringing my own. Every time I go to the loo a cloud of the evil little buggers rises from the bowl to chew at my bare flesh. I have so many bites it looks as if I've caught a strange tropical disease – 76 bites on my left arm alone, and I'm not even going to talk about my legs, feet and bum!

At breakfast once again we all wonder why the waiters in the restaurant are so surly, slamming down plates of food in front of us and greeting requests for more coffee with scarcely concealed irritation. And then one of the local writers explains to us that they haven't been paid for five months, with little chance to complain about such gross unfairness. Saddam might be gone, we agree, but corruption and exploitation are still rife, the norm rather than the exception, all making it even harder for ordinary Iraqis to believe genuine change has taken place and that building a new country is a possibility. Little wonder these unsmiling young men are feeling a tad hacked off; but at least if they keep on working, their families can still eat. I can hardly imagine what workers in the UK would do if they hadn't been paid for months on end but were still expected to turn up for work each day!

After breakfast Dr Ali says I should prepare for an interview with Iraqi tv in the main hotel building. It is a room with the largest chandelier I have ever seen; it's the size of a London bus, and probably costs enough to keep a whole village fed and clothed for a decade!! We sit on over-upholstered gilded chairs, and the walls are decorated with antique and modern guns - not my idea of ideal interior decoration or wall art. Fatma Naoot, the young Egyptian journalist is working overtime as translator, a job she undertakes with unflagging enthusiasm and professionalism.

Naturally the first question I am asked for is my impression of Iraq. I decide to be honest and tell them I am seeing a country decimated by decades of conflict that will take generations to recover, a broken country. Events like this Festival are important, a tiny shoot of optimism struggling for life and recognition in the debris of destruction that surrounds them, and something that might give local people a better sense of confidence for the future. That's why it is important for it to be supported.

And why did I think it was important to come here? I explain because in the UK so little is known about the country and its people; the only images we ever get on our tv screens or in the media are those of shootings, bloodshed, and soldiers at war. The message I want to take home is that there are ordinary people living in Iraq, people who are falling in love, getting married, having babies, going to work or school, and doing all the things ordinary people do everywhere…just trying to have a life.

And then they ask me to read one of my poems, not a full one, just an extract as interview time is running out. Fatma insists on a bit of my 'Shoes' poem – not what I would have chosen, particularly not with its overtly erotic sub-text, but I can't argue with her, and fortunately there's only enough time for the first two stanzas before filming has to finish. On the way out I am stopped by another film crew from a different channel asking me similar questions. Again, Fatma obliges with translation, and I tell them again how deeply affected I have been by what I am witnessing here, and the courage and strength of the people trying to rebuild both their country and their lives.

Interviews over, we go to a talk given by one of Iraq's most prominent women writers, who fled the country years before, leaving her family behind. Elegantly dressed in a pale green business suit, she explains that on one hot summer's night years before the shooting outside began again she hid in fear with her children. She put her hand up to her neck, she said, to discover it was dripping wet. In the darkness she couldn't tell if it was just her sweat, or blood, which meant she had been wounded. At that moment she knew she had to leave Iraq, and the very next day she began her journey into exile. That she is back in her homeland now after years of exile is a miracle, and she is filled with hope for the future, although recognizing it isn't going to be an easy or quick fix.

I wonder if the writers and poets from this troubled land will ever be able to stop writing about their bloody past and open the doors of their imagination once again so they can write stories about the future. But for today, Iraq's yesterdays are still too close, old memories are still too raw, the wounds are still healing, and there is too much grief and desperation to fill their poetry, novels and stories for the foreseeable future.

DAY FOUR – Monday, 7th May – Afternoon/Evening - Last Days and Children being Children

Now that all of us European writers have read our work, been interviewed to the point of overdose, had our photographs taken with what seems like half the population of Babylon, and seen the omnipresent effects of Saddam Hussein's atrocities, for the rest of our time at the Festival we only have to relax and enjoy ourselves. Jona and Tobias are planning to do a bit more traveling around Iraq, and as I listen to them discussing where they might visit and the best (and safest) ways of getting there, I wish I could travel with them.

I feel as if I have only just scratched the surface of this extraordinary country, and that it and its people have so much more to offer. Agreed, it's not the easiest or most comfortable place to go walkabout, but the sheer weight of history on offer here is overwhelming, an ancient civilization that should not be forgotten because of modern conflict. Iraq is a nation that has been demonized by the foreign media, by international politicians driven by their own agendas of greed and hypocrisy, and by its own inability to deal with its flaws (including extremists creating chaos for everyone living there). But I'm optimistic - the fact Jona and Tobias <u>can</u> travel to other parts of the country is an indication the wind of change is blowing across Iraq.

We go back to the Book Fair for the afternoon's last reading session, the Euphrates ambling sluggishly past only yards away. This time the readings are exclusively by Iraqi poets using a number of Iraqi dialects. We understand none of it, not even the multi-lingual Tobias, but just listening to the rhythm and cadence of another language unlocks a basic sympathy with the writer, and is a pleasurable experience in itself.

The emotional words roll over me, but I'm distracted by two little boys – clearly brothers – sitting next to me with their head-scarfed mother. They are both captivated by what's happening on stage even though they can't be more than 8 or 9 years old, clapping vigorously at the end of each reading. Although I doubt they understand everything they're hearing, their faces are alight with enthusiasm, their oil-dark eyes agleam. Yet when I laugh and say hello, suddenly they become shy and silent, hiding behind their mother's voluminous black wrap. She encourages them to say hello back. They retract even further. I hold out my hand in greeting, but they're reluctant to take it. Eventually mum decides a photo is in order, and the two of them are placed in a rigid pose either side of me while the picture is taken. I am the only one smiling, but mum is clearly delighted and beams at me widely before shepherding her two boys away.

After that we then move onto the readings at the arts centre across town. Although we still attract mega attention from local people who continue to gawp whenever we show our faces, after several days of our presence, the heavily armed guards at the door no longer take any notice of us as we walk into the building. Moammal, the Syrian calligrapher, corners me immediately with a shy smile and gives me a present…a copy of one of his beautiful pieces of calligraphy I'd admired the previous evening. I am touched he has taken the time and trouble, especially when it's unlikely we will ever see each other again. But if I ever do, hopefully I'll be in a position to buy one of his exquisite calligraphic art works.

The evening slides gently into darkness, and we listen to the remaining local and Arab writers who still have to read their work. Dr Ali's wife and mother come over to chat, embracing me with genuine warmth. His wife is a beautiful young woman with a perfect complexion and wide black eyes filled with gentle eagerness. Her sons surround us, all on their best behavior, but getting a bit tired of sitting still for so long. The youngest child is still a baby, his chubby little arms reaching up happily to whoever wants to pick him up for a cuddle. He clearly has no problem with being passed around like a fragrant parcel, and Jona happily bounces him up and down on her knee, laughing and cooing with him. I've never been that good with kids, so I watch in amusement.

And then we see a look on his little face, features red with concentration, that can only mean one thing when it comes to babies. Yes, he has pooped…onto Jona's leg, all over her trousers. The squirming infant, now looking much more relaxed, is handed back to his mum, who is mortified with embarrassment. She rushes off to find napkins and water to clean the mess her errant son has made of Jona's trousers. Jona and I are beside ourselves with laughter, and in only minutes the offending material is removed and all that remains of the 'accident' is a large damp patch on Jona's leg. Another international incident avoided!

Things wind up quite quickly after that, and we all head back to the hotel for our last al fresco meal. But Dr Ali has one last surprise in store for us. Each of us is presented with a special wood and plaster statue of a cuneiform tablet from the time of King Nebuchadnezzar, as a memento of our presence at the Festival. As each of us accepts our gift, there's applause, much laughter, and yet more photographs. But by this time, midnight is looming, and we're all a little too tired to continue being jolly. I know I have to be up dawn to leave the hotel by 5.00 a.m., and I still have to pack, so I bid a genuinely fond farewell to all the friends I've made during the past few days, and head off to my room. I want to thank Dr Ali for inviting me to be part of this extraordinary event, but he's disappeared...the Festival still has a few more days run, and he has a lot more to organize for all those artists arriving tomorrow.

I leave at 5.00 a.m. as planned for my early morning flight home. The day is already warming up as we head away from Babylon for the hour-long drive to Baghdad airport, the sun burning its fierce farewell in a clear peacock sky. The dusty palm trees and thorny scrub give way to barbed-wire-festooned concrete walls the closer we get to the city. I'm sorry to be going, though I am looking forward to sleeping in a clean bed where I won't be chewed by gluttonous mosquitoes!

Security at the airport is tougher on leaving Iraq than getting in, and I'm momentarily irritated at the endless body searches before check-in. The departure lounge is a bit too well-thumbed to be comfortable, its sparse shops not yet open. I ask myself if I've enjoyed the experience. Enjoyed isn't the right word, but it has been amazing, and I wouldn't have missed it for the world.

Would I come back? Yes, because there's so much more to see and experience in this place of poetry, deserts, conflict, disaster, atrocity, legend, ancient culture, and biblical riches. Because there are so many misconceptions I want, in my own way, to try and dispel. And because…I'm a traveler and this has also been part of my journey.

And then the flight is called. I gather my bags and head off across the cracked tarmac towards the waiting plane. I'm going home…

Going Back to Babylon in 2014 and 2016

Even though I was only there for less than a week, that first trip to Babylon to take part in the Arts & Cultural Festival was an extraordinary and eye-opening journey for me as a traveler and especially as a writer. Being invited to return in 2014 and 2016 consolidated all the things I had experienced and felt about the first trip, and I was eager to see the degree to which Iraq was changing, what improvements (if any) there were, and if the country was looking less crushed.

Happily, I noted that on each subsequent visit the security was less stringent, the accommodation less grubby, and the welcome by ordinary Iraqi's on seeing foreign poets and writers there ever more ebullient. Each Festival's programme followed the same kind of pattern, although it was rounder and more varied, with readings by various foreign poets, plus a broad range of writers from the Middle East and across Iraq, with enthusiastic arts-loving audiences for each and every event.

And we visited schools of the arts where young people were being taught dance, drama, music and all manner of creative endeavors, with equal enormous enthusiasm and dedication. The arts are definitely thriving in Iraq, and I still feel saddened that we in the West hear nothing about this positive side of life in a country still blighted by conflict and extremism.

We were also allowed to visit the summer palace Sadam had had built on top of the hill overlooking the town – a vast, brooding building that had obviously once been opulent, but was now scarred with graffiti and empty of everything except ghosts and dust. I had thought that the words scrawled across the spoiled walls inside the palace were slogans against the regime, but then discovered they were much more prosaic, of the 'Ahmed loves Fatma' variety…young people really are the same all over the world!

I've not been back since 2016 only because I've not had the time or wherewithal to get me there, but I know the Festival is still a highlight of Iraq's artistic calendar, still directed by the extraordinary Dr Ali. Hopefully at some stage I will be able to return, perhaps with this slender volume of work highlighting all the things I witnessed and experienced during my three visits. And I do really want to tell people that Iraq is an extraordinary place and that the western press should give equal mileage to its thriving arts and creative communities as well as to the conflict Iraqi's are so tired of.

Being there taught me so much, especially how lucky I am to live somewhere that isn't blighted by war - to know that when I make my way home each night, my home will still be there intact and waiting to embrace me.

Agnes Meadows - Biography

AGNES MEADOWS is a London-based poet/writer who has toured nationally and internationally, giving readings, workshops, and residencies all over the world, most recently in Bangladesh at the *Dhaka International Poetry Festival*, where she received a Literary Award for her contribution and commitment to poetry. She was a Guest Poet at the *Austin International Poetry Festival* for 10 consecutive years, twice winning awards for *Outstanding Writing*, and has read three times at the *Babylon International Festival of Arts & Culture* in Iraq. Agnes has written six collections of poetry, three with *Flipped Eye/Waterways*. Her last collection was a dual English-Chinese collection 'The Light On the Wall' (*Morgan's Eye Press*), from which she read at the *Formosa International Poetry Festival* in Taiwan in 2017. In 2019, she was invited to be *Guest Editor* of the *Atlanta Review Poetry Journal*, one of the world's foremost poetry magazines, focusing on the work of poets from or living in Wales or Cornwall. This edition will be launched in Spring 2020 and will feature the work of 48 poets. Since 2004, Agnes has also run *Loose Muse* Women's Writers Night in London, with regular satellite events elsewhere in England, and has advised Channel 4 TV on poetry. E: agnespoet@gmail.com

Palewell Press

Palewell Press is an independent publisher handling poetry, fiction and non-fiction with a focus on books that foster Justice, Equality and Sustainability. The Editor can be reached on
enquiries@palewellpress.co.uk